Who Do You Think You Are?

poems
Mary B. Gray

Copyright © 2022 Mary B. Gray
All Rights Reserved

Book and Cover Design: Rowan Kehn

Cover image: Augusta Savage's sculpture *Realization*, circa 1938. Federal Art Project, Photographic Division collection, circa 1920-1965. Archives of American Art, Smithsonian Institution, a photo by Andrew Herman, Archives of American Art, Smithsonian Institution.

ISBN: 978-1-7355762-8-2

Turning Plow Press

Praise for *Who Do You Think You Are?*

And this is why I call her Mother Mary! The truth in ink, a page turner of a poetry book. Plot twists to the left of me coupled with forgotten history to the right of me. At times the writer preaches, at other times she chants, and at other times she confesses. The writer leads us, she guides us to our authentic bloodlines, our rich history. This is the Black experience in America. This is America. We stand on stolen land. Then and now. The poems invite inquiry. The use of contemporary forms pushes us forward. The structure and content of this work could make one question: is this critical race theory in the form of a poetry book? They will want to ban Mary's works: A compliment.

This first book of poetry is for the lifespan. A gift for grandchildren and grandparents. American fact.

—Gay Pasley, progressive activist, writer, and photographic artist

"Our stories must be told" ends the poem "Augusta Savage: In Her Hands," and in this dynamic debut collection, poet Mary Gray does exactly this, telling stories of African American lives from myriad perspectives through her artful, musical lines. Bass Reeves, Augusta Savage, the Fultz quadruplets, Michaela DePrince, Doris Payne, and Michelle Jones are some of the more famous figures who appear alongside girl scouts, WW I soldiers, the poet herself, hiplet dancers, and victims of police brutality. Gray makes this polyphony of voices cohere through her elemental, mythological language as well as her deft use of rhythm, rhymes, refrains, themes, and forms. At the same time, she uses these voices to explore concepts such as freedom, violence, duty, self, family, country, and pleasure that are often less than coherent, especially given African American history, which is synonymous with American history. In sum, this collection provides real knowledge, shining beauty, and disciplined hope.

—Timothy Bradford, author of *Nomads with Samsonite*

Acknowledgments

Thank you to my family for making me who I am: Darlene Gray, Fred and Anne Gray, David Gray, Jackie Green, Laswanique and Clifton Mayo & family, Darrell and Karen Gray & family, Daniel and Sharleigha Dickey & family, Michael Lewis & family as well as the Taylor family. I also want to dedicate this collection to loved ones I have lost: Betty Gray, Brenda Lewis, Mary Feathers, Cora Feathers, and Walter Taylor.

Special thanks to the most loving people I am honored and humbled to call my friends: Jennifer Foster Cowns, Tiffany Sokica, Tiffany Leindl, Lucy Burke, Rachel Wood, Kayla Watkins, Chemere and Thaddus Molden, Ashlea Gause, Francine Baker and Renee Pedersen.

Thank you to my co-workers for their enthusiastic interest in what I do outside the office.

Thank you to Short Order Poems for making me write spontaneously and on a typewriter.

Thank you to the members of Deep Deuce Writing Society for bringing me back to writing when I needed it.

Thank you to John Selvidge and the Ralph Ellison Foundation for the opportunity to teach what I love.

Thank you to Hank Jones for pushing me to publish when I wanted to quit and introducing me to Paul Bowers and Turning Plow Press.

Thank you to Paul Bowers and Turning Plow Press for hearing my voice, publishing this collection and helping me accomplish a dream.

Thank you to the Scissortail Creative Writing Festival for cultivating a vibrant festival for writers and readers.

Thank you for the author photo by The Billy Green Photography.

Special thanks to Jessica Isaacs and Gay Pasley.

To the Red Earth MFA students, graduates, professors, and my mentors Timothy Bradford, Jeanetta Calhoun Mish, and Allison Adelle Hedge Coke I owe immense gratitude for inspiring me to write again and to write fearlessly.

"Little Girl Blue" and "Girl Scouts of America Get a Colored Troop, 1917" were previously published in *For the Sonorous*, Issue 2, November 2017

Contents
I.
Bass Reeves Flees 3
A Chant for Nellie 5
Nellie Reeves' Calling 6
A Father's Love 8
A Real Lawman 9
Girl Scouts of America Gets a Colored Troop, 1917 10
Dorothy's Musings While on Stage 11
Augusta Savage: In Her Hands 13
Street Urchin 15
Green Apples 16
Ondria Tanner and her Grandmother, 1956 17
Black Children with White Doll, 1942 18
How Much? 19
A God Among Babies 21
Mary Catherine 23
The Quadruplets 24
Sam's Chamber 26
June Gibbons to Her Twin:
    To Her Twin from Jennifer Gibbons 28
The Orphan's Ballet 30
The Art of Stealing 34

II.
Who Do You Think You Are? 39
A Good Year 41
A Mother's Loving Libation 43
Little Girl Blue 45
Vacation Bible School 47
The Difference a Little Moonlight Makes 48
To A Cheating Man from his Girl 49
A Prayer on Hefner 50
NAACP Issues First Ever Statewide Travel Advisory 51
Getting Home 53
The Officer's Memory 55
Recalling the Night 56
Everything Can Be Weaponized 57
Educators Fail to Embrace Black Students' Hair 58

Hiplet: The Ballet Disruptor 60
Doctors in Training 64
A Second Chance 66
A Poem for Senate Minority Leader Mitch McConnell
    on the Eve of His Unrealized Faux Pas 68
The Politics of What Ifs 70
Confessions of a Dash Cam 72

I.

Bass Reeves Flees

An escaped slave, Bass Reeves would become the first black U.S. deputy marshal in 1875.

lookin' back across the
territory line   the Arkansas river
at my back   I shoulda known—
i'm a slave (now fugitive)
so I must be a cheat
Master Reeves named the game
five card stud   believed he
was the biggest stud on civil
battlegrounds still fully clad
in gray uniform trimmed with yellow—
the mark of a cavalry colonel
his chest still bloated
each round he bet each round
I followed lost sight of
my master's pride
that black king hidden
in my mind's eye
only revealed
to claim my winnings
I took the pot   I took his pot
but I should've known
what's mine is his   what I am is his
i'm a slave (now fugitive) so I must've
cheated   swindled   taken his blows?
like the property he thinks I am
but a man can only take so much
I'm a slave and a man
but he can't call me no cheat

gave him my fists for my honor
fugitive   fleeing   fled
a free man into the tall grasses
of the Indian plains

A Chant for Nellie

Outside Seminole warriors dance into the night
in step with rhythmic drum beats
their horses' hooves almost shuffle in step
crickets chirp callin'
for their other halves
everything lit by dancin' embers glowing
my mind should be on keepin' the peace
yet inside this tent
all I can do is chant her name

    Nellie   Nellie   Nellie

I long to dance around her fire
I will go home to her
travel back from territory trails to Nellie

How can a man dance
when he's so far from his woman
Inside here all I do is weep her name

    Nellie   Nellie   Nellie

Whispers of statehood on political lips
promising away tribal lands
don't stir up more passion than her hips
for all I can do now is whisper

    Nellie   Nellie   Nellie

Nellie Reeves' Calling

Bass Reeves wed Nellie Jennie in 1863, and she raised their eleven children on the Arkansas homestead.

an honorable man
needs an honorable wife
and my man has me

he finds his way back
to the house he built
all eight rooms with

his own bare brave hands
he returns after weeks
trackin' those outlaws

all across God's plains
back to our homestead
and find his house be tended

his bath be drawn
his children never be underfoot
let my man rest

cause a honorable woman
knows her honorable man
carries more weight

and worry of wrong and right
on his shoulders than
a hundred scoundrels combined

when he gets home
make sure I am willing,
able and *ready* to please

when he fall to sleep
his chest my pillow
I breathe him all in—

the smell of sweat
and I know the wild
still lingers here

he a changed man
I hear his hardening
heart beating in the
jail of his chest
unable to rest and I

just want him back
on the farm again
being my man

A Father's Love

Benjamin "Bennie" Reeves was born in 1880 and convicted of murder in 1902 after his father searched, found, and brought him to justice.

I'd been runnin'   hidin'   runnin'   from a lawman
prayin'   it ain't my papa chasin' the scent of fugitive
chasin' the scent of his own flesh and blood
I ain't never seen that man rest
in all my twenty-two years not when he
trackin' a killer not when he, sensing my deceit
whooped my ass for taking what was not mine
I knew he'd be searchin' for me with twice that force
'cause spilled blood stains deeper than spilled milk
but when a woman lies with another man
not once but twice a mild man can take
matters into his own hands seeing red spillin' red
my misdeeds papa can't overlook
then again he might be a sight for bloodshot eyes
a pair of loving arms to fall into as I become a child again
after a scraped knee   maybe I become his child again
forgiven thru my father's love

A Real Lawman

they say the lone ranger
was based on me Bass Reeves
others say that can't be
the way I see it that ranger is
the myth of a lawman
storied by some suits
sitting on their seats
in the Motor City
seeking to fascinate folks
over the airwaves they
ain't know nothing
'bout bein' a peace officer
enforcin' the law
ain't like nothing in those
buttoned up tales
see I rode the roughest trails
west of the Mississippi
bested outlaws more
savage than any rabid
beast in the wild and
I never wore white
that'd be too tidy for
long days turned to long
nights following the
foul odor of outlaws
running for their lives
too tidy for the blood
stains a peace officer
collects I ain't no
legend just a lawman

Girl Scouts of America Gets a Colored Troop, 1917

What they goin' teach me
that ain't already in my blood
My ancestors drank from the gourd
followed that star straight to freedom

In my blood I already know which berries
fill bellies and which berries are better
left alone   mama taught me
her mama taught her   all the mamas
right down that plantation line

They gonna teach me courage   confidence
and character but visions of granddaddy's
lashed back taught that long ago
We separate but equal in our
pleated skirts and tied neckerchiefs

We good enough to camp and scout
in our very own troop now but we can't
sing   or march   or camp
with the little white girls—their confidence
their courage   their character must
stay pure of this colored skin

How they goin' teach me to sing
when I've heard spirituals so
heavenly God still wonders why
us black beauties haven't reach equality

Dorothy's Musings While on Stage

Legend has it Dorothy Dandridge, the first African American actress to be nominated in 1955 for an Academy Award for Best Actress, dipped her toe in a segregated hotel pool.

A year ago, one sweltering summer day
over in Sin City, they wouldn't have me
in their hotel pool. Condemned me to stay
in quarters made for those with brown skin.

But I escape into the devil's heat, bikini clad
while white onlookers gasp and gawk
as I move closer and closer to the pool's
edge, dipping one colored toe into cold
cold chlorinated water.

Water I later see drained way away.
Had my brothers and sisters on their knees
scouring,
scrubbing,
cleansing
all my negro germs way away.

I heard an earful from
Mr. White Manager too
screaming the pool isn't for *my kind*.

What *kind* am I? An actress?
A dancer?   A singer? The entertainer—
Tonight, behind the hotel stage
his tone has changed.

Beneath sounding applause—
profound praise.
It changes little.

Enter through the back door, passing
powder rooms for white skin only
staying hidden way away
until I'm on their stage.

Too black to do
much more than sing
and still too black to
plunge into their cold
cold chlorinated water.

Augusta Savage: In Her Hands

in Clay County Florida
I went to the earth
to find clay to make my brothers and
sisters from clay to make
life-like figures
    so   so   real
at times even I look twice

daddy prayed to his God—
"rid his wicked girl of her ways
her false idols   her graven images"
but still I molded them
modeled ever still in His image

art cannot be dissuaded
moldable clay begging to be formed
a human harp lifting every voice
to sing the stories of brown-skinned
men   women   children
    such a realistic representation
societal stereotypes
should cease to stand

with my brown hands
I sculpted out a place
for my race in art history

no more rotund
Aunt Jemimas,
Rastus or Cooky's
darkened as midnight
mouths agape flapping
round red lips in the wind
casted in the shadows

of apes no these images
don't form from my clay

see these humane
depictions   offerings of humans
so long animalized
trivialized   debased
defined by the absence
of right white

but in new light   the renaissance
in Harlem echoing what I long knew
there is art in our skin
our stories must be told

Street Urchin

After The Gamin, *a sculpture by Augusta Savage*

my nephew, disheveled
displaced, everything he
owned carried on flooded waters
'cept for the shirt on his
back, the trousers around
his waist, wrinkled
relocated, him and all
our kin, up north
from dusty dirt roads
to a concrete jungle
my apartment crowded
ten bodies deep he
escapes out into
those windy streets
if I dust him in bronze
paint his skin into the
plaster the cast as
heavy as hurricanes
will it capture
his sufferings
if I reproduce
replicate him—
them each a
representation a child
aging hardening
in some city street
will the world see them?

Green Apples

After the sculpture by Augusta Savage

my body weeps from hunger
nose upturned phantom fragrance
guiding my nostrils
forward another day
each step a lightened memory
staggering steps
syncing with growls festered
deep within my belly
rumbling reminders of the empty
depth of myself
I keep my hands close, fighting
not to release the reverberations
so they do not hear what
can already be seen
in the outlined bones
plastered with brown
thin paper skin
I am like Adam, my body naked
only God gave that son sweet
green apples
saccharine juices spilled from
his mouth and he was full
in a bellyful garden he
hungered no more
while I still move in famine

Ondria Tanner and her Grandmother, 1956

A gigan after Ruth Ellen Kocher
and the photograph by Gordon Parks

Grandma gonna buy me a dress
a plaid blue one a new one

clean up real nice   dress up real nice
put the hot comb thru tough tufts
I promise not to jump I'm a big girl now

make it slick   straight   shiny like grandma's hair
just like the white mannequin dolls

that don't look my way they don't look
out the glass to see my faded red dress

but soon I'll look just as pretty as them
grandma gonna buy me a new dress

slick my hair straight like grandma's hair shiny
each hair perfectly in place just like the little
mannequin girls living in luxury behind glass

grandma says we window shoppin'
she gonna buy me a new blue plaid dress

Black Children with White Doll, 1942

*A gigan after Ruth Ellen Kocher
and the photograph by Gordon Parks*

for the picture man, I grab my finest doll
my only doll, sally, we sit against the wall

she and me are pals, I put my arm around her
lean in and whisper to smile for awhile
there's a camera let's show some style

her face doesn't change it never really does
when daddy came home told mama he lost his job

sally stared with blank eyes even when tears fell
from mama's eyes then junior's eyes then mine

she's really a witch, I hate her so, but mama said
for the picture man grab your finest doll

her face doesn't change it never really does
even in the night when I reach for her, cold
I know her eyes are blank mouth in a frown

she's probably daydreaming of some little girl
who looks like her, pretty, in a house in town

How Much?

babies in glass rooms cannot throw stones.
how much to see the black quadruplets
in the window? the first identicals of their
kind made 1946 right here in the US of A.
how much to see the black quads
in the window? oh you'll have to ask
Dr. Klenner their self-proclaimed
unofficial guardian. he brought them
into the world, pulled them from their
brown, deaf-mute mama over in
the basement—the negro wing.
named them instead of their share—
cropping daddy. in hand Klenner returned
with Mary Ann— named
after his wife, Mary Louise—named
after his daughter, Mary Alice—named
after his aunt, and Mary Catherine—named
after his great aunt, harkening back
to a time when slaves were named
by their owners. how much to see the
black quadruplets behind the glass?
you'll have to ask their doctor—
guardian— owner, I do believe they can be
gawked at for the right price:
visitors are welcome at the home
between 2 and 4 p.m. each afternoon.
the quadruplets can be seen
through the glass walls. those
dark darlings bathed in light fetch
a pretty penny! Pet Evaporated Milk
pays the good doctor— their selfless,
unofficial guardian so they'll appear in ads
and if he gains a little money and fame
a mouthpiece to promote his

vitamin C therapy then that's *his* business,
so how much to see those
black quads in the window?

A God Among Babies

I build my empire on the backs
of babes. Four identical little black backs,
just sturdy enough to hold my weight.
Medically speaking, they are
a miracle and I, their messiah.
A doctor among negroes— their only hope
I break bread in the basement,
willing myself to first do no harm.
I glove my gifted, white hands working to
separate mother from babe one,
separate mother from babe two,
separate mother from babe three.
A doctor with less mental fortitude may have
stopped there but my instincts know
triplets are quadruplets. Four identical
black girls 3 pounds apiece. I bring them
into the world saving their
little lives. All without the proper
equipment in the basement negro ward.
Their little limbs lingering, shaking
in the absent of light.
I wrap them in cotton gauze and
huddle them for warmth like little
Jesuses had his skin been marred black
and he duplicated four times. I save their lives,
birthed medical wonders. I name them
cause their mama mute could not should
not take credit for such a feat. The babies
need a proper guardian, their daddy
only a tenant farmer with a mess
of children already back at home.
I look after them when the vultures
come calling, their liquid tongues
confusing lesser brains. I read

over their contracts, keep those babies
off their mama's worn, sagged breasts
keep them growing on dry milk
keep them strong with my trusted
vitamin C regimen. Lead them on
tours across the land, traveling black sisters
given a pass to lead parades, grace
magazine covers, meet President JFK
all things because I brought life.
On the backs of babes I build my empire.

Mary Catherine

The last Fultz quadruplet born cemented her and her sisters' fame as miracle multiple babies.

I came into this world unexpected
a kept secret started in one womb
hidden behind one   two   three sisters
mirrors reflecting me for a moment
then I was alone   unknown

My sisters a world away, they in life
lungs inflated deep underground
I waited for one sister   two sister
three sister wails   signaling
all clear   I cross over unborn to born
reuniting our quartet

underweight underneath artificial
lighting we grow into small wonders
under artificial concern our stories
travel first by lips   then by press
four identicals born and alive

a brown one
a matching brown two
a duplicated brown three
an unexpected brown me
a miraculous feat

The Quadruplets

1.
Mary Louise:
We are souls enslaved as sisters,
born in sameness, interchangeable
never drinking our mother's
natural milk instead
we are Pets of
advertising, a living exhibition
while cries escape
our lips and dried
milk fills our bellies

2.
Mary Alice:
In front of lens we grow from
flower girls identical
down to the last relaxed curl
white-gloved teens the lawn
our stage White House backdrop
a sideshow that can
travel anywhere

3.
Mary Ann:
as women the charm of
our uniformity fades
finding no public eyes
scanning the factory floor
for four identical quadruplets
fashioning raincoats

4.
Mary Catherine:
I am the unexpected one,
the last one born,
the last one standing
my sister Louise the first subtracted
only aged 45 succumbing
to breast cancer the
clock ticks five years
subtracts my sister Ann
alike in death just as in life
the clock ticks five years
my sister Alice—they the
expected triplets now
all gone leaving only
the unexpected one
this time I do not follow

Sam's Chamber

During World War II, the US military secretly tested mustard gas and lewisite on black troops to determine their effects on black skin.

He wanted me, my Uncle Sam
to be all I could be, I enlisted

but standing in the chamber
I thought
Uncle Sam ain't my kin

My skin bubbles
in a heat hotter than Hades

heaving in the chamber
I see
the door has no knob

we could melt
into puddles of flesh

Sam wanted to know to win the war
to see if this brown hue
proved chemical resistant

for why else would God make blacks
but to be ideal chemical soldiers

our skin meant to
endure the unseen
flames test cases
meant to save
white lives from
the front lines

kneeling in the cage
I realize we
blacks are weapons
the Japs don't have

soldier subjects sworn
to secrecy we
served with scarred skin

June Gibbons to Her Twin:
To Her Twin from Jennifer Gibbons

Known as The Silent Twins, June and Jennifer Gibbons born in 1963 only spoke to one another until Jennifer's death in 1993.

I hate my sister twin
She, the antagonist
I, the protagonist
entangled storylines
hers overlapping mine
with her thorned vines
In my mind, full length
novels longing for singular
adventure a solitary existence
she reads me with telekinesis
cryptophasia   she tells me I am hers
we walk in synchronized steps
I think she is mine but she came first
so she must lead
making us of one mind
something split
in two and shared
a piece for her
the other for me
the bond of a twin
there is never quiet constantly she
talks in my head   everything I
think she feels
we are one not two we are merged
her life an affront against mine
she strolls the ocean floor
depressive—a temperament
I must share we lie catatonic
I think to move   she hears me

dissuades me a cheating
woman   why should
she drain my light   my life
this is not the first time a queen
a tormenting tyrant
must be dethroned and beheaded
our life's rising action
to a formidable climax
I think she knows   she
must die

The Orphan's Ballet

*a PechaKucha after Terrance Hayes for ballerina
Michaela DePrince*

I.   *First Position*
in the beginning love   in the beginning
بابا (papa) ماما (mama) a small family
no sooner than the days turn
there is no one   The Orphan's Ballet

II.   *Elancer*
you cannot flee war when war mars your birthright
nothing can grow   flourish from hate   from a distance
men battle for power   create rivers of blood

III.   *Second Position*
we stand in line for food   for clothes   for toys   for love
last in line receives nothing   there isn't enough to extend
reach   orphan twenty-seven   I must grow full
on my dreams

IV.   *Etendre*
Ballerina   the word fills my mouth *bal-ler-rin-a*
later I will thank Magali for capturing everything
I will one day be in '79   traveling to '98   for me
foreseeing my fate

V.   *En Pointe*
tiptoes meet barren ground, bare feet on unforgiving earth
mere practice for the densely packed layers of fabric
cardboard   glue imitating   imitating   imitating
her posture imitating her smile even in pain

VI.   Derriere
our teacher   is lifeless now   rebel soldiers
machetes in hand bet on the unknown   what is now
known   an unborn baby girl spares neither life

VII.   Relever
to rise up would be to float again on the air of esteem
owning this patterned skin   believing happiness awaits
outside these gates   across the ocean

VIII.   Third Position
hands held high *en couronne*   can the devil's child
be gifted a crown? can a spotted leopard dance with grace?
I say yes one day I will be Tchaikovsky's queen swan

IX.   Sauter
I leap on strong legs   legs born to jump   to the heavens
land back on disrupted land   my fingers brush
heaven's floors   and I am transformed

X.   Fourth Position
Feet together   overlapping the most natural state
of being   the natural state of loving   laughing
learning this is life seconds in infinity

XI.   Glisser
one must move swiftly   I move like the leopards
every step is purposeful each step confidence
no time to follow uncertainty
these moves are the mind's extension

XII.   Fifth Position
Twenty-six overlaps me   her reflection her experience is
my own my experience   number twenty-six does not lose
her laugh   taken together   sisters born of tragedy triumph

XIII.   Tourner
pirouettes   in the spin there is nothing but my force   wind
little tornado   turn   perpetual will   turn   gather speed
turn   turn   turn   stop on my mind's command
I am force

XIV.   Devant/en face
black cannot be clean   pure   white
black cannot dance principal   black can fade away up-stage
but this black has endured too much and come
too far not to own this stage

XIV.   Pas de chat
I embody the animal whose spots I wear
cat-like movement intrinsic quality of
the spots they shame   but only I know I am
fierce like the leopard and so I will dance

XVI.   En evant
forwards and onwards   orphaned child must turn
back eyes on me   eyes on me   I am not the devil's child
I am in light   I am light   forward

XVII.   Jeté battu
and my legs flutter like angel wings   a move of
abounding joy for now there is no suffering   there is no
war there is no orphan   alone   only flutters of hope

XVIII.   Plier
to bend is to fear   to fear is to be human
to be human is to trust   I trust again as I bend
to brush the wood below me   there is nothing to fear
here   there is nothing to fear

XIX.   De cote to left
homes left have been torched   possessions I left
behind ashes   yet I phoenix   I transform   I am ballerina
dancing outside myself   one step left

XX.   De cote to right
dancing my body rejoices to the right   to the righteous
have been given family   friends   faith again
everything is now right   with one step right
I dance out   everything is now right

The Art of Stealing

As a prolific jewelry thief, Doris Payne's career has spanned six decades as she began to practice the art of stealing at fourteen.

1. Persuading in Bloomingdales

I radiate my golden hue
gleaming your reflection
brown on your skin sugar
I spark compulsion
in your eyes and I see
you need golden me
Unfasten my clasp
make me pocketed property
22-karat body all yours
this heist our secret
like a stolen kiss between
forbidden lovers

2. White Collar Crime

Draped in a designer dress
I float through Saks Fifth Avenue doors
through Cartier's doors through
Bloomingdale's doors
I am Audrey Davis, the bride of
a prominent lawyer, I am
Thelma White, well-to-do
Socialite, I am Sonya
Dowels, wealthy widow
causally confident I charm
open jewelry displays
I try on one ring then
another slip off one try

on another then a bracelet
some earrings slipping items
on and off with such speed
waiting for any distraction
a customer, a phone call
a dizzy spell I help
myself to jewelry seen
in Town & Country magazine
make a pocketed purchase
before politely handing back
everything promising to
purchase another day I
smile demurely exiting as
I entered, afloat.

3. *Payne's Jewels*

Cool gold around my brown wrists
more brilliant than handcuff shines
          I risk everything

I risk everything time and time again
compulsion to prove everyone wrong
          They never expect me

They never expect the elderly
I smooth talk   spellcast
          then I am gone

I'm gone with my dimes still in my pocket
newly adorned in fine jewels
          I'm wrapped in luxury

I'm wrapped in luxury around the world
Greece, France, Britain   I've fooled the Swiss
          living under assumed names

It's glamorous   this lifestyle of mine
          I've no regrets
          I've no regrets

II.

Who Do You Think You Are?

Cindy Crawford traces her roots

learns she
                descends from Charlemagne

This sparks my curiosity

I need to know from whom I
                          descend

am I the distant relative of an African King

                          a civil rights activist
a Harlem Renaissance artist

so I shovel out 100 bucks for an Ancestry.com subscription

    I knew it would work

    I prayed it would work

But I never

        find my way
                    back to African shores

only make it back to Louisiana

        as far as my great-great grandmother

and the traces of her parents

        her roots
    their roots

the records

everything to ashes   descendants fated to flames in some

                              town hall records room

Who do you think you are?

        As far as I know
        I descend from Charlemagne and Nefertiti too

A Good Year

It's a good year   nineteen ninety-three or five or
or four & my only worry is a field of green
green grass sprinkled with more candy
than my young eyes can see
to honor the Easter bunny   or the women & men
working hard on the assembly line
forming rubber to wheel
but my only worry is the other children
eyeing the lot of loot

fall in Oklahoma & I barely feel the winds
my shoulders support a canvas newspaper boy sack
now my costume my grandma's work wear
my mother's work wear but not until morning
when they wrap sack and gently
rest the city's daily news on
neighbors' front door frames   but now it's Halloween
and I walk the streets ironically collecting candies
from neighbors' doors   later we meet grandpa
at the coliseum   with those other tired
mamas   and daddies   and uncles   or aunts
but it's still a good year   at the fairgrounds
the rides a respite from
those night shifts   those day shifts
every child's only concern   this child's
only concern   filling my plastic bag
with more & more sweets

nineteen ninety-something & the good year
is coming to a close   ice weighs down
the town and my grandpa waits with
corporate-sponsored Santa but I'm not bothered
my eyes are fixated on a mountain of toys
contemplating what I will carry home oblivious

when grandpa slips away back to work
a black Barbie doll within my grips
It is a good year

A Mother's Loving Libation

the sirens will wail
three minutes 'til noon
and grandma's mind lingers
on her twins miles away
states away countries away
she seeks out
plastic liter jugs full of water
she has lined
neatly along the porch

pouring one out on the steps quickly
two minutes before noon and
the air will fill our ears with alarm
keep the evil away and
protect uncle Darrell and
uncle Daniel

one minute before noon
the water eeks it's way along
expanding in
this tornado-less day   this is just a test
but a stream is formed in her
concrete desert waterfalling
down
down
down

finding dirt earth
her prayers now intermixed
into God's creation
her small ceremony over
settling her mind and heart
if only for another day

until she has her boys home
again safe again as if they
were twins in her womb again

Little Girl Blue

Little girl blue
never blew her horn
a trumpet that came all the way
from south Texas
found its way to little girl blue
in 6th grade (when she stood hardly five-foot-two)
the grade they introduce musical instruments
into the lives of youths
form bands all across Oklahoma lands

Little girl blue wanted to play the clarinet
it was a cute instrument   black
slender   with polished keys
like all her friends
but Grandma stuck her with the horn
worn brass she could barely grasp
'cause it was already in the family
wouldn't cost to buy or rent
she settled for what was sent
where is the girl with the song so soulful

Little girl blue figured she'd play some blues
after she learned the scales of course
put her lips to brass   and that little girl
blew   and blew   and blew
'til her cheeks couldn't take no more
waited for a note to escape the bell
the trumpet didn't yell
so her eyes fell,
she looked to the band director   searching
searching for an answer
why couldn't little girl blue blow the blues?

Mr. Band Director looked her square in the eyes
diagnosed the problem as too big lips
Little girl blue never blew that horn again
had it sent back down south

Little girl blue fast asleep
will they wake her, will she get woke
you see she hadn't yet heard of
Louie   Dizzy   Tiny   Valaida
didn't know there is no blame
no shame in luscious large lips
Little girl blue never blew no horn

Vacation Bible School

Oklahoma heat outside
but I'm inside the air conditioned
love of the lord   I vacation
in baptist brimstone and fire
travel under empyrean methodist skies
holiday in the pentecostal isles
grandma says his love is always free
activities even we poor can rest in
so I sing his servants' songs
of Abraham   of Zacchaeus
of Noah and Jonah
and I sip sweet scarlet Kool-Aid
construct paper-mache crosses
popsicle crosses
crosses made of beads
all in remembrance of sacrifice
I still don't understand

The Difference a Little Moonlight Makes

In figurative moonlighting
        underneath radiating stage lights
Barry Jenkins, director, artist, black man,
        lost something
        won something
        then lost something again—a moment
a time in the spotlight for him and his all black cast
their limelight stolen, replaced with artificial lighting
the tremors of awe from Barry's wildest dreams
stolen by some accountant with the wrong envelope
too smitten by Stone's crystal bronze
gold dress against pale perfect skin—
the gold standard in Hollywood's hills and academy votes
in the time of #OscarsSoWhite
instead his earned awe surrounded in spectacle
"This is not a joke Moonlight won Best Picture."
"This is not a joke Moonlight is the Best Picture."
"I think you guys should keep it any way"
says the host who lives in
a La La Land where all that appropriated jazz jumps
and little black boys and brown girls   stay marginalized,
get gaslit   their own spotlights
dimmed while taking center stage

To A Cheating Man from his Girl

For Leon Bridges in response to his song "Better Man"

I didn't need much
thought you weren't a cheating man
thought I was your baby
gave you my good love so,
sent you off   singing on stage for those
jezebels the smell of their lust only faintly
covered by cigarette smoke
thought I'd be the only woman
under your silk soft scarlet sheets
you've got a smile too crooked, blackened heart
it was never love, I was never enough

What can I not do? What can I not do?

Give you back my heart
You could catch pneumonia
swimming that temperamental
muddy, greenish orange Mississippi river
it wouldn't be enough to give you another start

Remember I was up all-night pacing 'til
morning heard the sun say good morning
when you finally staggered home

Boy, the subject's still tender no knelt
pleas of longing from your desert will
open my well

What can I not do? What can I not do?
Forgive a cheating man

A Prayer on Hefner

Driving toward red and blue flashing lights
I merge left to pass by   a black couple
pulled over for some perceived offense I do not know
my chest tightens as I
merge left to pass by   three cop cars
pulling them over for some perceived crime
do their hearts too race
I do not know   so I pray
be calm
be compliant
be careful
but, God, is that enough?
It wasn't enough for so many others
I cannot even whisper all their names
I pray those officers   aren't trial   aren't jury
aren't executioners dressed in sheep skin
pray my fears aren't realized today
pray I'm not witness to the beginning
moments leading up to endings
I pray the evening news doesn't headline
Cop involved shooting on Hefner Road

NAACP Issues First Ever Statewide Travel Advisory

209 miles away by car
I could travel northeast
on my way to my aunt and
uncle in Illinois see my
cousins only 6, 9, 12
in 2017 just passing through
Missouri where driving while
not white traveling while not
white vacationing while not
white appears suspicious
I wonder if I could do anything
while black in Missouri
my 2012 Chevy has no cruise
control my lead foot could
easily push 1 mile over the
posted speed limit then sirens
flashing red and blue lights backdrop
the flashbacks of 31 years
Trumped up charges could cost a
lifetime in a jail cell like Tory Sanford
who asked police for help
while running out of gas while
black in Missouri. He just got
lost on his way to Nashville the
father of 8, jailed for unrevealed
reasons died in a cell in some
unknown small town alone could

my fate be his fate
never arriving to my destination
never arriving to my family
only arriving to the end of me
life while black in Missouri[1]

---

[1] This poem was written as a mixed media poem after Harmony Holiday and originally is depicted on a collaged photo with the June 7, 2017 travel advisory over a 1961 photo of Civil Rights activist Priscilla Stephens being arrested by white officers.

Getting Home

Son was there ever a way
to get back home?
when brothers in blue
see black but not you
was there ever
a way to get back home?
when conceal carry civilians
see black but not you
was there ever a way to get back to me?

my boy tonight I cannot
sing you to sleep I must
sing you awake

brown boy   brown boy
you're going to carry
that weight your whole life

it's a part of you
carried in skin
that someone said sinned
against God and
got marked dark

that was what was said
when your ancestors
became property
labored in fields, yielding
nothing for themselves, not even
the guarantee to live another day
a weight carried for generations

there was never a way
to get back home
when you are caged within a
black skin you didn't choose
you make do   you make good

but little brown boys
like you don't make it home again
little brown boys don't make it home
their mamas watching streetlights
becoming spotlights becoming flashing lights
and they know there was never a promise
their sons would come home

The Officer's Memory

gun smoke in the night air
fills my nostrils I'm transported
backwards into boyhood
into a humid heat
crouched in what seems like
the greenest brush my brother
an arm's length away my
daddy two arm lengths away
my granddaddy three
arm lengths away
all of us in the still quiet
in my scope bear black
strolls in the grass
like an oversized man
I hesitate finger on the trigger
one moment too long
before the crack echoes
before the bear black
leaks crimson stumbles along
then a timbering fall
chastised by generations
my brother takes my kill
I'm only left with
the smell of smoke
then I'm back in the night
the sound of screams
pierce me from my dream
and all I smell is iron
as his body leaks red
now a man I never miss
I shoot to kill always
claiming my prey

Recalling the Night

lights fill my rearview
mirror like a sunrise
only flashing my heart
races faster than the 25
mph speed limit I never
exceeded a knock on
my window forceful thuds
fill my ears where
radio music now fades
I lower the window
its mechanical hum
brings in icy air
behind his badge
he tells me
step into the night
to step into compliance
around these impoverished streets
he is the law and he knows it
perverted power
behind his smile
in the night,
he likes the way
the moon illuminates my brown
nipples hardening in the cold
he grabs his gun tells me
it's loaded before
letting me off
with a warning

Everything Can Be Weaponized

knives, guns, bombs, fear, cars,
education, elections, the worldwide
web, shelter, planes, viruses, vaccines,
food, the media, men, anger, insecurity,
knowledge, xenophobia, children,
light, trains, homophobia, legislation,
women, weather, bacteria, semis, toxins,
our bodies, food, freedom, history
tasers, fire, trucks, love, baseball bats,
badges, racism, the environment,
sexism, tanks, prisons, money,
music, religious intolerance,
water, hate, hair, privilege
in the wrong hands or even in the right hands
everything can be weaponized

Educators Fail to Embrace Black Students' Hair

Young black girls going natural
taking the big chop
shedding the weight
hair long damaged
long conformed
straighten to the standard of so-called
splendor their *unruly* hair needn't be
straight chained by
heated iron combs
chemical *relaxers*
(first made to
lubricate machines)
flat irons for them
to conquer the classroom
be scholars
become tomorrow's entrepreneurs,
singers, explorers, politicians,
doctors, coders, thespians
lawyers, athletes, artists,
designers, builders, creators
mothers be strong and proud
in their
natural, found in/produced by nature
faux locs, afro, twists
box braids, spiral curls
dreadlocks, frohawk,
cornrows, TWA (teeny
weeny afro), twisted
pompadour, havana twists,
corkscrew curls
springy curls, close crop 'do
senegalese twists, mirco braids
twist out, bantu knots, coils

wash and go out
into the world unapologetic

Hiplet: The Ballet Disruptor

a PechaKucha after Terrance Hayes

1. Hiplet
classical ballet too refined for black skin   no more
trained us in grace Homer's vision of
African dance so rap ballet begets
hip-hop/rap ballet begets   hip-hop ballet
begets   hip-let begets
hiplet   a black empowerment movement

2. En Pointe
moves so fierce   only my toes grace the earth
every step an attitude   professionally trained
we innovated the game   self-defining   hip-hop on pointe
slip in and out: classical   urban   classical   urban

3. the Tootsie Roll
it ain't the butterfly   it's the tootsie roll   legs in and out
work them hips a lil'   put some hood in it
a touch of the street the music   lures the hips
fully embodied feministic fairy with cred

4. the Cam Cam
ballet arms floating through the air
body becomes fluidity when the beat drops
feet scrap the floor   legs kick up like a bull
they came for swan lake

5. the Sexywalk
sexy skin in all shades
work the runway
slay the catwalk
vogue strike a pose

6. the Soutenu Scoril
latin flavor en pointe   salsa   samba
sustained spin sexy   spinning sexy
gathering force like a tornado   spin   strong
self-assurance sustained   spin

7. the Hiplet Strut
Head held high   though they would have you
hang your head in shame in your skin
give them a hair flip   the metaphorical middle finger
this stage turned runway   move with attitude

8. the Twist In & Out
on tip toes twist in triumph
turning to the world to say we're still here despite
our skin successful still   standing strong
we celebrate unashamed

9. the Moonwalk
on the smallest of bones I glide   a nod to Michael who wowed
them all then—black and white like now
you see they did not know
black girls could hold so much grace   land on the moon
and transcend to a valued space

10. the Zippy
elegance in grace   black is bright   fresh
lively leaving sprinkles of life black does
not scorch the earth   elegance in grace
makes new   makes fresh

11. the Body Roll
our bodies long ago learned to roll with   the hate
stereotypes entrenched in myths made to diminish
baby mama drama   vexing video vixens   black loud angry
we say, no!   we roll   we rise   we rock

12. the Part of Array
worlds intertwined   what is art if not worlds merging
revealing parts   shining rays of shape   body
type female   elements emotions   old new made contemporary
keep communities relevant   keep kids training for more

13. the Walk
each step fire   attitude swan lake never called for
classical with a shake a   shimmy
channeling Checker a twist on a twist

14. the Jump
jump   we might as well find greater height
ascend invisible despite heavy chains   change the narratives
dance diverse skin into forbidden spaces   jump

15. the Turn Up
arms extended all the way to the sky ending in a fist   fury
a force swaying   swaying   sway still on pointe
step touch   step touch

16. the Bourre
traditional ballet feet in fifth move in quick
motion mix eye catching revolutionizing
a merge so quickly caught in trend   a hashtag a craze
to praise somehow still amazed   we create

17. the Vivian
we know what Aunt Viv knew in Bellaire
black women have grace, have attitude
a finger snapped pay homage   hips bounce our arms
outstretched   slightly bent flapping   we fly

18. the Charleston
steps steeped in black history   when they had nothing
to dance for   fast kicking step   throw the feet forward
and back and just for good   measure stay on your toes

19. the Confidence
flexibility in form   freedom to express
with no regret   to dance
unapologetically in any space   explore and soar
grow gorgeous generation unashamed our skin

20. the Movement
our bodies move to own rhythms
in a culture that would rather forget
than respect any woman of color
in this space tights come in all shades of
brown   center stage our legs no
longer hidden within pale pink tights

Doctors in Training

Possibly swayed by false beliefs about biological differences between white and black people, some white medical students tend to rate the physical pain of a hypothetical African American patient as less severe than that of a white patient in the same circumstances, says a study published in the journal Proceedings of the National Academy of Sciences.

our blood is the same
lungs   liver   heart
all the same
pain   pain   pain
doctor   I have pain
examine my skin
brown juxtaposed with
your skin white
foreign to you this
skin different is
brown skin thick
strong collagen alligator
this black skin like porcupine
quills or work horses back
on the plantation taking
a lash and then back to work
it's evolutionary
you believe blacks
just don't feel pain
lacking scientific proof
prescribe beige band-aids

In the next room
a patient presents
the same symptoms
same blood
lungs   liver   heart
wrapped in white skin
In your medical opinion
whites cannot endure such pain
pull out pad
prescribe pain pills
but like Baldwin said
you are the *real* victim
of your own brainwashing
clinging to your myths
our brown skin
holds no hatred
no hatred

A Second Chance

For Michelle Jones

Before Harvard's rescindment letter
after Harvard's acceptance letter

before repaying her debt to society
after spending half her life

rehabilitating behind bars,
before applying to graduate school

becoming a published scholar in
American history behind bars

without internet access instead
searching through the photocopies

of historical archives tracing
the origins of her involuntary home

before making a promise to herself,
to him, to live a redeemed life after

becoming prisoner 970554, sentenced
to 50 years before being found guilty

by a jury of her peers for neglect
and murder only after confessing

her crimes during a stay in a mental
facility, before the baby's daddy

questioned the boy, his boy's whereabouts
before her son was never seen again

before regaining custody
of Brandon from his grandma and his dad

before her boy got taken
by the state because

she was too unfit, too unequipped
to raise a special needs child alone

before she gave birth at just 14
before her mama took a plank to

her well-formed, rounded belly
after she confided her worst fear

and secret shame before she
was sexually assaulted by

a high school senior who
stole her innocence

well before any jury
passed judgement

when was the right time
for a second chance?

A Poem for Senate Minority Leader Mitch McConnell on the Eve of His Unrealized Faux Pas

After Sojourner Truth's speech 'Ain't I A Woman'

Am I not American?
I was born in the great state of Oklahoma.
You remember? The one taken from indigenous hands.
Did my grandfather and his sons not serve this country
representing its interests domestic and abroad?
Are they not American?
Do we not have birth certificates that state this fact?
Do we not have those social security cards you
used to keep track of those American born
(it doesn't even say we're black)
So are we not American?
Did I not see the Challenger explode?
Feel bombs reverberate through sweeping wind
down Oklahoma plains?
Can I not remember exactly where I sat
when the weight of the Towers falling onto
American soil shook from coast to coast border to border
And when we mourned together as one nation
did my tears stand out among the stream—
as an outsider looking in?
Am I not American?
Have I not eaten apple pies
or prayed under Friday night lights?
Have I not voted (because if you don't vote you can't
complain, but those with brown skin we shouldn't complain
be grateful for our scraps)?
Have I not paid my taxes-- financing governmental
programs--even the personal passion projects
of lawmakers just up to no good?
So I must ask, am I not American?
Have I not recited our preamble?

Have I not saluted our flag pledging my allegiance?
Have I not sung our anthem reaching
for impossible notes with professional provision?
Have I not studied our history as
whitewashed as it may be.
So can I even say 'our'
or is my equal ownership still in question?
am I still not American?

The Politics of What Ifs

had the Xbox not been stolen
perhaps Charleena would not have
phoned 911 for help and
had she not lived in a complex
for people transitioning out of homelessness
and had she received mental health counseling
(but only if it wasn't a secret shame for
women of the black community)
had she not had a previous skirmish with officers
had that encounter not ended with the charge
of harassment of law enforcement
and obstruction of a public official
had she previously handed over her child
without incident
had she not had an officer safety tag
assigned to her name
had they not had their preconceived notions
had they warned her they would shoot
if she had not held kitchen knives one in each hand
or scissors that time before
if 4 out of 4 of her children had been home
instead of just the 3
had her pregnancy been further along than
just three months (but they say human life begins
at conception) perhaps if the young officer
hadn't forgotten his Taser
or had the Seattle police policies overhaul been
successful after the DOJ called them out for
excessive deployment of force
perhaps, maybe she would have lived to celebrate
her favorite holiday (just two weeks from her death)
captivated her family with goofy charm or fun loving
dance moves maybe her children would not
be motherless, would be awaiting the arrival

of a little brother or sister, and perhaps one more
black family could have gone unbroken

Confessions of a Dash Cam

Based on former Police Lieutenant Greg Abbott's comments caught on Dash Cam during a traffic stop as reported by many news organizations and "The Raw Videos That Have Sparked Outrage Over Police Treatment of Blacks" *as tracked online by* The New York Times.

Underneath a starless, draped sky
cars move rhythmically down
the highway in Marietta, G.A.
and a dash cam video apprehends
a moment: modern model
car, silver, under
patrolling headlights, a
passenger bone stiff
too paralyzed to even motion
for the phone in her lap:
"I've just seen way too many
videos of cops…"
The officer's reassuring:
"But you're not black.
Remember we only kill black people.
Yeah. We only kill black people, right?
All the videos you've seen, have you seen
any white people get killed?"

You are not Richard Hubbard III
of Euclid, O.H.
it's okay to reach for your phone.
You are not Demetrius Bryan Hollis
in Lawrenceville, G.A.
it's okay, reach for your phone.

You are not Nania Cain
from Sacramento, C.A.
reach for your phone.
You are not Dejaun Hall in Vallejo, C.A.
It's okay.

You are not a fifteen year old
featherweight freshman
black girl body slammed
against the floor in Rolesville, N.C,
where buyers once travelled by train
to shop the slave market.

You are not Jacqueline Craig
handcuffed with her
teenage daughters after
reporting a neighbor's
punishing hands around
her 7-year-old son's small brown throat
just for dropping a wrapper—a littering criminal
in Fort Worth, T.X., home
to the largest Civil War Museum
south of the Mississippi.

You are not Charles Kinsey in
North Miami F.L., a mental health
therapist lying on his back,
with hands held high
shot in the street
near his client with autism
a scared young man with
a toy truck cradled
in his hand.

You are not Keith Lamont Scott
in Charlotte, N.C. waiting
in the wrong parking space
at the wrong time, shot at his
own apartment complex
his children's bus stop
within eye distance.

You are not Terence Crutcher
in Tulsa, O.K., in need of
car help and drug habilitation,
unarmed
but looking like
a *bad dude* with his hands in
the air before he is shot.
It's okay.

About the Author

Mary B. Gray, a poet since she learned of poetry as a child, was born and raised in Lawton, OK, and currently resides in Oklahoma City, OK. She received her Bachelor of Arts in both Journalism and English Writing, as well her Master of Public Administration (MPA), from the University of Oklahoma and her Master of Fine Arts from Oklahoma City University. Mary has taken part in Short Order Poems and The Ralph Ellison creative writing workshops. Previous public readings include the 2018 Martin Luther King Jr. Day of Celebration, Society of Urban Poet presentations in 2019 and 2020 as well as the Mark Allen Everett Poetry Series in October 2019 and the 17th Annual Scissortail Creative Writing Festival in 2022. Her work has been published in *Ain't Nobody That Can Sing Like Me: New Oklahoma Writing*, *Territory Magazine* and *For the Sonorous*.

www.ingramcontent.com/pod-product-compliance
Lightning Source LLC
Chambersburg PA
CBHW020546080526
44583CB00013B/1024